Christmas in England

by Cheryl L. Enderlein

Content Consultant:
Peter McInally
Assistant Press and Public Affairs Officer
British Information Services

Bridgestone Books

an imprint of Capstone Press
Mankato, Minnesota

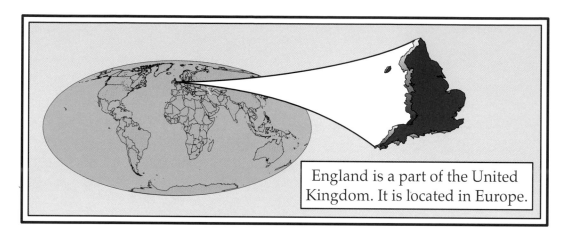

England is a part of the United Kingdom. It is located in Europe.

Bridgestone Books are published by Capstone Press
151 Good Counsel Drive, P.O. Box 669, Mankato, Minnesota 56002
http://www.capstone-press.com

Library of Congress Cataloging-in-Publication Data
Enderlein, Cheryl L.
    Christmas in England/by Cheryl L. Enderlein.
    p. cm.—(Christmas around the world)
    Includes bibliographical references and index.
    Summary: Briefly describes the customs, songs, foods, and activities associated with the celebration of
Christmas in England.
    ISBN 1-56065-624-7
    1. Christmas—England—Juvenile literature. 2. Christmas decorations—England—Juvenile literature.
3. England—Social life and customs—Juvenile literature. [1. Christmas—England. 2. England—Social life
and customs.] I. Title. II. Series.
GT4987.44.E53   1998
394.2663'0942—dc21

    97-11340
    CIP
    AC

Photo credits
The Hutchinson Library, cover
Tony Stone Worldwide/Kim Christensen, 4
Trip Photographic Library/H. Rogers, 6, 8, 12, 14, 16, 18, 20; M. Peters, 10

2 3 4 5 6 04 03 02 01 00

Table of Contents

Christmas in England

Christmas is a holiday that is celebrated around the world. Celebrate means to do something enjoyable on a special occasion. People in different countries celebrate Christmas in different ways.

England is a part of the United Kingdom. The United Kingdom is located in Europe. People from England are called English. They also speak English. Their Christmas greeting is Merry Christmas or Happy Christmas.

Many North American Christmas traditions come from England. A tradition is a practice continued over many years. One tradition that started in England is sending Christmas cards.

Christmas Day is December 25. The weather in England is usually damp and cold. One old English tradition was lighting a yule log. A yule log is a big piece of firewood. People burned the log to celebrate Christmas.

People in England decorate for Christmas with lights.

The First Christmas

Many Christmas celebrations are part of the Christian religion. A religion is a set of beliefs people follow. Christians are people who follow the teachings of Jesus Christ. They celebrate Christmas as Jesus' birthday.

Jesus' mother was Mary. She was married to Joseph. Mary and Joseph traveled to the city of Bethlehem. They could not find any room at the inns. An inn is like a hotel. Mary and Joseph had to stay in a stable. A stable is where animals are kept.

Jesus was born in the stable. His first bed was a manger. A manger is a food box for animals. The manger was filled with straw.

Wise men brought gifts for Jesus. They followed a bright star. The star led them to Jesus.

Many Christmas celebrations remind people of the first Christmas. Many English people celebrate different Christmas traditions.

People in England set up figures to remember the Christmas story.

Symbols of Christmas

Christmas crackers are special Christmas symbols in England. A symbol is something that stands for another thing. Christmas crackers are small tubes covered with colorful paper. They are not food. They are called crackers because they make cracking sounds. They make the sounds when they are opened. The crackers remind English people of a crackling fire.

There are surprises inside each cracker. The cracker pops open when the ends are pulled. The surprise falls out. Crackers usually hold a paper hat and a small toy. They also have a joke in them.

Everyone receives a cracker at Christmas dinner. It is placed beside each person's place. Christmas crackers were created by Tom Smith. He started making them more than 100 years ago. Christmas crackers are a special part of Christmas in England.

A Christmas cracker is placed beside each person's plate.

Christmas Celebrations

One English celebration is called Boxing Day. It is the day after Christmas. Boxing Day is not about fighting. The name comes from collection boxes at churches. The boxes were used to collect money for poor people. On December 26, the church leaders would open the boxes. They would give the money to needy people.

Today, people celebrate Boxing Day by going to equestrian events. Equestrian means having to do with horseback riding.

Boxing Day also starts the season of pantomime. A pantomime is a play for the whole family. The name is often shortened to panto.

Actors perform pantos at theaters. They tell stories like fairy tales in a funny way. There are many jokes and songs. The people watching the panto cheer and boo. Many families go to the panto every Christmas season.

The season of pantomime begins with Boxing Day.

Decorations

People in England decorate their houses for Christmas. They put up Christmas trees. They decorate the trees with lights and Christmas ornaments. An ornament is a decoration hung on a Christmas tree. Some ornaments are colored balls and stars.

Christmas trees are evergreens. Evergreens are plants that are always green. They do not change colors even in the winter. A long time ago, people believed evergreens were magical. That is because they were always green.

Other types of evergreens are mistletoe, holly, and ivy. They are used to decorate people's houses. Mistletoe has rounded green leaves and white berries. Holly has sharp green leaves and red berries. Ivy has pointed green leaves but no berries. Evergreens are important Christmas decorations in England.

English people decorate Christmas trees with ornaments.

Santa Claus

The first Santa Claus was a man named Saint Nicholas. A saint is a special person in the church. Saint Nicholas lived a long time ago. He secretly gave gifts to children and poor people.

Today, people in many countries believe in a Christmas man like Saint Nicholas. The Christmas man in England is Father Christmas.

Father Christmas has a long white beard. He wears a long red coat. Sometimes he wears holly on his coat. Father Christmas is tall and thin.

For the past 100 years, the idea of Father Christmas has been changing. He is becoming more like the North American Santa Claus. Father Christmas arrives on top of houses in his sleigh. A sleigh is a sled usually pulled by animals. Father Christmas' sleigh is pulled by reindeer.

Father Christmas is the English Santa Claus.

Christmas Presents

People all over the world give gifts at Christmas. Giving gifts reminds Christians of the wise men's gifts. The wise men brought special gifts to Jesus when he was born.

Children in England believe Father Christmas delivers presents. He comes late at night on Christmas Eve. He waits until everyone is sleeping. He comes down the chimney. No one sees him. Father Christmas fills all the children's stockings. The stockings might be hung on the fireplace. They can also be hung at the end of the bed. Sometimes children put out pillow cases instead of stockings.

English children like to write to Father Christmas. They write him letters about the gifts they want. In the past, the children did not mail the letters. They threw them up the chimney. Today, there are fewer chimneys in England. Children send letters to Father Christmas by mail.

Children receive gifts from Father Christmas on Christmas Eve.

Holiday Foods

Stir-Up Sunday is about five weeks before Christmas. English people make Christmas desserts on this day. Some favorite desserts are plum pudding, mince pie, and Christmas cake.

Plum pudding is made with spices, nuts, and fruits. It was made with plums. Now, people use raisins instead. They put a coin in the pudding. One person finds the coin at Christmas dinner. English people believe finding the coin brings good luck.

Mince pie is a small, round pie. It used to be made with meat. Now, it is made with fruit and nuts. Christmas cake is a fruit cake covered with a candy layer. Icing covers the candy. The top is decorated with plastic Christmas figures.

English people usually eat turkey, potatoes, and brussel sprouts for Christmas dinner. Brussel sprouts are round, green vegetables. After dinner, people eat desserts made on Stir-Up Sunday.

English people make Christmas desserts on Stir-Up Sunday.

Christmas Songs

Many English people sing carols at Christmas. A carol is a Christmas song. Groups of people singing Christmas songs are called carolers. Carolers go from house to house singing. Some people invite the carolers in to visit or to eat. They offer the carolers hot drinks or money. English people believe caroling brings good luck to homes.

Choirs also sing carols during the Christmas season. A choir is a group of people who sing together. Some choirs give Christmas concerts. Many of the concerts are given at churches.

Another old tradition is wassailing (wah-SAIL-ing). The word wassail means to your health or be whole. Wassail is also the name of a hot apple drink. People used to take a bowl of wassail to their neighbors. They sang a special wassail song. Then they went inside to drink wassail together. Few people practice wassailing today.

Some choirs give Christmas concerts at churches.

Hands On: Make Christmas Cards

The first Christmas cards were made and sent in England. You can make Christmas cards to send to your friends.

What You Need

Different colors of construction paper

Glue

Things to decorate your cards. You can use glitter, ribbon, lace, paint and sponges, old Christmas cards, magazines, and other things.

Markers

What You Do

1. Pick a piece of construction paper. Fold it in half.
2. Decorate the front of your card. Here are some ideas.
   - You can use pictures from old Christmas cards or magazines. Cut them out and glue them on.
   - Cut a sponge in a Christmas shape. Dip the sponge in paint and stamp it on the paper.
   - Use lace, ribbon, or glitter to make a Christmas design. You could also use construction paper or fabric.
3. Use the marker to write on the inside of the card. You could say Merry Christmas and sign your name.

Words to Know

carol (KAR-ruhl)—a Christmas song

choir (KWIRE)—a group of people who sing together

Christian (KRISS-chuhn)—a person who follows the teachings of Jesus Christ

equestrian (i-KWESS-tree-uhn)—having to do with horseback riding

evergreen (EV-ur-green)—a plant that stays green all the time

inn (IN)—a place to sleep overnight like a hotel

manger (MAYN-jur)—a food box for animals

ornament (OR-nuh-muhnt)—a decoration hung on a Christmas tree

stable (STAY-buhl)—a building for animals like a barn

yule log (yool log)—a big piece of firewood

Read More

Cuyler, Margery. *The All-Around Christmas Book*. New York: Holt, Rinehart and Winston, 1982.

Fowler, Virginie. *Christmas Crafts and Customs*. Englewood Cliffs, N.J.: Prentice-Hall, 1984.

Lankford, Mary D. *Christmas Around the World*. New York: Morrow Junior Books, 1995.

World Book. *Christmas in Britain*. Chicago: World Book, Inc., 1978.

Useful Addresses and Internet Sites

The Embassy of the United Kingdom
3100 Massachusetts Avenue NW
Washington, DC 20008

British Information Services
845 Third Avenue
New York, NY 10022-6691

Britain in the USA   http://britain.nyc.ny.us
Christmas.com   http://www.christmas.com
Christmas 'round the World
http://www.auburn.edu/%7Evestmon/christmas.html
A Worldwide Christmas Calendar
http://www.algonet.se/~bernadot/christmas/info.html

Index